27.50

RMA
Darjeeling
x,/76

BUDDHIST POEMS

Other works by the same author

Buddhism
A Buddhist Students' Manual
The Buddhist Way of Life
Concentration and Meditation
The Field of Theosophy
Karma and Rebirth
A Popular Dictionary of Buddhism
Sixty Years of Buddhism in England, 1907–67
Studies in the Middle Way
Teach Yourself Zen
Zen Buddhism

BUDDHIST POEMS
A Selection, 1920–1970

Christmas Humphreys

London

Published for the Buddhist Society by
George Allen & Unwin Ltd
Ruskin House Museum Street

ISBN 0 04 821026 9

Printed in Great Britain
in 10 point Times Roman
by W & J Mackay & Co Ltd, Chatham

CONTENTS

A book of Buddhist poems should contain poems of Buddhist in-
spiration or at least on a Buddhist subject. It may be that after some
fifty years' immersion in Buddhist belief and practice I tend to look at
most things with a Buddhist eye, and many of these poems are admit-
tedly brief articles on Buddhism in verse. Indeed, I am frequently told
that I say more and far more deeply in a page of verse than in a dozen
pages of prose. With me both forms of writing are highly compressed
and in verse, which allows one to by-pass many of the laws of syntax
and logic, the meaning is conveyed, if at all, by an excess of elision
which amounts to a series of skips and jumps. But have I not heard
somewhere of an existential leap into Reality?

Here, then, are Buddhist verses chosen from the product of some
fifty years, and ranging in form from the close-wrought shape of a
sonnet to the loose texture of 'Lines in Firelight'. But verse has rules
as well as a language of its own. The rhythm which would destroy a
passage of prose, and the ornaments of metre, assonance and rhyme
are alien to the later, for it is the later form of writing. True, Yeats
began *The Oxford Book of Modern Verse* with a passage of Walter
Pater's essay, 'Leonardo da Vinci', in which he sets out the phrases in
verse form and presents the result as a poem. But then Pater is said to
have written each sentence on a separate piece of paper. Others since,
submitting their work as poems, have done no more than to cut up
tolerable prose into lengths. But is the product verse and, more im-
portant, does it anywhere rise to the level of poetry? For I submit that
poetry is not so much a form of words as a hard-earned compliment
paid to a piece of writing usually in verse but sometimes in the 'purple
passages' of prose. A poem in my view is a fusion of inspiration and
expression which reflects the fusion of spirit and matter central to the
mind of man. Poetry can never be defined, but it is the indefinable
element in a set of words which makes it valuable and memorable,
and a worthy addition to the art and craft of literature. Without it
verse should not be described as poetry. A craftsman of words can
create fine verse which is devoid of the least spark of poetry, and the
distinction should be as clear in the reader's mind as sadly obvious to
the poet.

How shall one test a set of verses for the presence of poetry? I
proffer three lines of enquiry. One may test with the simile of light, for
a poem or part of it 'lights up' when the clay lamp of verse is visited
with inspiration. Another simile is elevation, for the 'lift' when the

divine afflatus comes is almost physical. I remember Roberta Shuttle-worth saying a long time ago, at the Poetry Society,

> A poet is troubled with these two things,
> The presence of feet and the absence of wings.

Most verse, alas, never leaves the ground.

A third simile is that of music, for surely a poem should sing, whether the song be a ballad or a hymn, a dirge or a lyric, or just a paean of joy. Rhythm, rhyme and assonance, and the delicate delight of well-wrought vowel-sequence and grouped consonants, these pertain to the music of poetry; the factors of light and lift reveal the spirit of man in the workshop of his choice of words.

The light may be a blaze, in one of the immortal poems of our language, as found and rightly so in most anthologies. Or it may be a rich glow shining through the vesture of a longer work. The lift may come at any time, as in the opening of the sestet in Rossetti's 'Love-sight' or in Keats's 'On First Looking into Chapman's Homer', or it may, though seldom, be maintained throughout a major poem. At times the metaphors of lift and light may combine in that of a mind illumined by the raising of consciousness just so much nearer to the light within. Few poets can so rise at will; the many are at the mercy of inspiration, itself the breath of life breathed in.

Some write poetry all the time, as Rupert Brooke even in the frivolous nonsense of his letters home from Tahiti. Others, as in the polished steel of Flecker's work, still show traces of the midnight oil. Some burst out at high level and manage to stay there, as in 'Everyone Sang' of Siegfried Sassoon, or preserve an agony of mood as in Tennyson's 'Break, break, break'. A few, as my claimed re-discovery, Gerald Gould, sing gently in the mood of love, or with a cry as in Francis Thompson's 'Arab Love-song', and occasionally words can produce the very sound of music as in the tolling bell of Christina Rossetti's lovely 'Remember me'.

All this is possible in mere blank verse. What finer poetry by any standard than in a thousand lines and more of Shakespeare, whoever used that name, or in the Tennyson-Malory splendour of 'Morte d'Arthur'? Indeed, the verse need not be decasyllabic, and I have long been jealous of Henley's remarkable 'Margaritae Sorori'. But surely the more free and lawless the texture of the product the more difficult it is, bereft of rhyme and metre, to produce a masterpiece, and how rarely is it done.

But poetry is not a matter of purple passages, whether these be sneered at as 'romantic' or loved as things of beauty ever present at one's side. We need but return to the low-pitched key of Tennyson's 'Lucy' or Dowson's 'O Mors!' to see how far these are from the embroidered glory of Thompson's 'Hound of Heaven'.

But I have erred. What folly to talk of the great poems in our language before presenting my humble own! Yet before a tribunal of my fellow craftsmen, including members of my own generation who loved and sought to imitate the forms of old, I would submit that the following verses do contain a few poems judged by the high standards here displayed. It is for the reader, if such poems exist, to find and enjoy them.

Some of these poems appeared in *Poems of Peace and War, Seagulls,* and *Shadows* published during the war by the Favil Press; in *Via Tokyo* (Heinemann, 1948), in the third edition of *Studies in the Middle Way* (Allen and Unwin, 1959) and in *The Buddhist Way of Life* (Allen and Unwin, 1969). Others appeared in the following periodicals: *The Aryan Path, Chambers's Journal,* the *Daily Graphic, The Middle Way,* the journal of the Buddhist Society, *The Occult Review,* the *Poetry Review,* the *Sunday Times* and *The Times.* I am grateful to all concerned.

The Buddhist poems may be vaguely grouped as the History of Buddhist Thought, Basic Principles, the Self, Karma and Rebirth, and Zen, although not written with any such thought in mind. The rest need no analysis, for Nature, Love and War have ever been the themes of poetry.

T.C.H.

St John's Wood
15 February 1971

The pinnacles of Buddhist thought contain perhaps the highest achieve-
ment of the human mind. The doctrine of the Void is ultimate, empty of
all 'things', even of emptiness, leaving only THAT, *the Namelessness.*
The following eight poems seem to be concerned with these heights of
thought, however named.

In Search of Nothing

Why look for it? Why seek it? Why demand
Of each unravelled semblance this one thing
Which none has seen nor yet can understand?
We crave possession, comfortless; we cling
To blind enquiry, hope that in some phrase
Or virgin book or teacher's mouthing mind
The hot hand of pursuit, in sudden blaze
Of splendour will magnificently find
And hold it to the heart forever . . .
                                        Fools!
It is, and is not found or bought or given.
Effort, enquiry, search, these are the tools
Of revelation. Not in earth or heaven
Shall self, my self, ravish the final veil
And, kneeling, see the face which has no face
To see with, nor self-purpose to prevail.
Yet in that moment when the hands of space
Close to the compass of a point, not here
Not there, and time sleeps uninvented . . .
                                        So,
The senses shall not find it anywhere.
'It lies within.' Oh clouded saying, No!
What of the host without if this within
Is sole and royal servant of the Light?
Is earth we know a darkened wheel of sin,
And heaven alone the dim-illumined height?

It lives and moves. It changes not. It is,
Within without, to all men visible.
In laughter, love and in our vanities

It is, divided, indivisible.
Is is beyond, and more. It has no being,
No hands of action, no disturbing will.
It sees and knows, yet no thing sees in seeing.
It is the whole of all yet each thing still.
It shines in no-self-ness, in right endeavour
Fades when the one is falsely rent in two.
It waits, a moment stretched into forever,
Far, far beyond the reach of me or you.
Why seek it, then, in market place or mind?
Let it be lived and loved and deep enjoyed;
It is, we are, with nothing left behind.
How rich it is that owns and is the Void!

The Void is Full

All is a thing which is not something else.
(All that is something else is also a thing).
All things are void.
The Void is the name for an absence of all things.
The Void is also full,
Full of No-thing-ness only.

To see

To see that there is nothing; just to see
No thing. The inward eyes are stopt, confused
With errant views of unreality:
Of birth, uprising and mortality
Of circumstance; of garments daily used
For mutual appearance; of the warm
Communion of friendly hands and eyes
That seeking answer smile, and seem to form
The substance of things other.
                              Lies, all lies!

Nor born of God nor yet phenomenal
Here's no thing utterly, no thing at all.

And I, that wakening perceive no thing
Am to the thing unseen invisible.

Here's void of emptiness, a mind awing
Serene of difference and answering
To no compulsion of a thought divisible.

The seer/seen is not, and I to know
Must, void of vision, see them wholly so.

Translated from the Japanese, Jijimuge *means 'the unimpeded inter-diffusion of all particulars'. A central doctrine of the Kegon School of Japanese Buddhism.*

Jijimuge

Each thing of beauty, each unlovely thing
Is other, every other, but the mind,
Thought-laden, ego-burdened and confined
With difference wrought of false imagining,
Is million-eyed to broken circumstance
And mirrors all in multiplicity.

Yet each is utter each, complicity
Of substance fusing life; no child of chance
But rightly thus, and lit with suchness, such
Beyond of difference as silence knows,
Or love, that lingers in the heart's repose
While master of the tools of sight and touch.

Each thing is void, a flung thought of illusion,
Yet dwells in unimpeded full diffusion.

Look Down to Heaven

Look down to Heaven where the limbs of man
Must writhe and sweat in bondage to be free.
Look down, for there alone and visibly
Lies the wide ambit of a godless Plan.

Look down and be unfriendly to the high.
All thought so pinnacled has neither stuff
Nor present volume. Scarce it shines enough
To mirror forth our insufficiency.

Look round. In here and now the roving mind
Consumed in pain and bound in nescience
Creates with vacant eyes all consequence,
And cries aloud in fetters self-designed.
Look round, and see drowned faces of despair
And lightless hands that fumble and forget
Their provenance, Here's flame of Hell.
                                        And yet
Behold within the riving darkness there,
Pervading all the heart with sudden glow
A new-lit lamp, awareness wakening
To self-perception, shining thoughts awing
Of new-born immanence. Not yet to know
The Limitless, but such a sword of light
As pierces all distinction, flows and fills
The darkling caverns of the night and spills
Upon the far shores of the infinite.
Here's Heaven, here in this and very now:
Not ultimate but touchable, not stilled
With thought of death's cold permanence, nor filled
With hopes impalpable. The sky-flung vow,
The panic prayer that leaps from impotence
Is now without, and Heaven, ultimate
On earth, unrolls from human lust and hate
To laughter born of vision, an immense
Uprise of impulse surging to attain
The light now bright within. Here sudden joy

With hands of love is instant to employ
Devices ocean-wide to heal the pain
Of fellow man's begetting. Here the mind
Knows the beyond of knowledge, and the heart
Is live aware of each unsevered part
Of Wholeness.
                    Heaven is here for each to find
In service of the child in need, mankind.

Always Today

Always today, that knows no different hour,
I see the bud, the full unbounded flower,
The drooping head and death upon the ground.
Always today the mountain range is drowned
Beneath the waters whence it strove to climb
In many-millioned cycle of no time.
Always today.

There is no past; the past has ceased to be.
No days to come; they are not presently.
No journey hence, no traveller, no Goal,
No polishing the foolish brick of soul.

Only today,
The day that is for ever here and now
Of labour in fulfilment of no vow,
Of Life that is itself the only Way,
Always today.

A Rose is Absolute

A rose is absolute; not evidence
To man of life's impermanence,
That all that grows must fade and fall.
It is a rose, a scented absolute,

Itself entire, and not a mute
Appointed symbol of the All.

I too am absolute, that silent stare
Intense of will, importunate
Until with voided mind, heart-consummate,
Sudden I shall be wide aware
And know, as all creation knows . . .
A rose is absolute, and I the rose.

The true Buddhist is not confined to the language of any one religion for expression. This is in Christian terms, but is none the less sound Buddhism of the Mahayana School.

Full Cycle

God, to know himself as God
Breathed and produced a Son.
And all that is, or great or small,
Is member of that One.

And each is Self, unsevered Light,
And every Self a flame,
And you and I, the eyes of God,
Are Self without a name.

But in the Darkness yet unseen
And now as yet divine
The voice of folly cries aloud
'I am, and this is mine'.

And so we suffer, self-deceived
And bitterly complain,
Until we rise and take the road
From God to God again.

This and the following nine poems reflect long years of study of the basic principles of Buddhism.

Rootless Thought

We've lost our first beginnings, the great power
Of wonder and amaze. Intemperate thought,
Boastful of each precision concept wrought
Must wither, as a rootless, severed flower
When ravished and bereft of nourishment.
The conscious heart, a lotus on the pool
Of unawareness, with compassion full
And void of difference, is well content
To feel the sun of life, the wind of pain
In all things visible, softly to kneel
Before the truth in myth enshrined, to heal
The wounded soul with symbol, and retain
The motherhood of earth.
                              Proud thought alone
Is barren, breeds but thought again, and dies
Before the Namelessness, whose naked eyes
See utterly the faceless Known-Unknown.
Only the heart, the spirit's lantern, knows
The root and holiness of thought awing,
The splendour of the spirit's flowering,
The dawn wind and the summer rose.

Release anew the springs of life; drink deep
The wisdom that we do not know; arrest
The flight of self in gilded thought expressed,
And in the wholeness of becoming reap
The guerdon of humility. Then mind
And heart, the intellect a proven tool
In service of the One Unknowable,
Shall climb beyond and seek and haply find.

Suffering

To suffer is to suffer well, to accept
The untoward circumstance, to bear with skill
The weighted balance which the fool, inept
In equilibrium, would strive to kill
With flight or malediction. Would he thrust
With hand of will the pendulum of rule
From powered harmony, the law is just
And swings upon the wise man as the fool.
To receive, to suffer wholly, to digest
The living deed's implicit consequence,
Here's error's absolution; full confessed
The deed dies in the arms of immanence.
To suffer is to grow, to understand.
The void of darkness holds a proffered hand.

Open the Door

(On hearing the Appeal by the Rev. Austen Williams for the St Martin-in-the-Fields Christmas Fund, 1970)

Open the door, and let the sick world enter in.
Here is no private place, no citadel.
The body's pain, companion till its end;
The riven heart of grief
That utterly may share no friend;
The violent mind in unrepentant cell
All these shall enter in.

Open the door. Let hunger in;
The prisoners of silence and the blind;
Disease unsociable, and limbs that crawl
Once proudly used; sad men that fear
Pursuing hands for follies criminal;
And those of clouded and uncertain mind;
All these shall enter in.

Fling wide the heart. All men are suffering.
All men are suffering and all are you.
Pay gold to oil the wheels of charity,
The debit of the heart remains,
Of common woe of all men's causing,
Each one the loser as the debt falls due.
All men are suffering.
Open the doors of self, your self;
Hate and illusion closed and shutter them.
The key is love that uses ageless words
On lips of love that utter them.

The doors flung wide, all battlements dissolved,
Compassion with her infinite devices flows
And floods the arid mind with love.
Then suffering, the lonely debt
Of deeds that knew not love, shall prove
Its provenance, desire with self its cause.
Mind will deny its fathering;
The heart's compassion knows.

True love is void of self and suffering.
We have not found it yet.
Open the doors.

I suffer, we

I suffer; others suffer. Are there others
To ourselves that cry aloud in pain?
We are issue of one Father, brothers
Of a lone begetting, born of the Unborn,
Opposing enemies as Abel/Cain.

We strive with our relations of like blood,
With blind futility moving to gain
Advantage. Joined in separation, torn
Asunder, the whole plenitude

And spawn of life's paternity is slain,
Yet comes again to battle, wins and dies,
Or losing all yet lives. And each at feud
For ever kneels in self-abasement, wise
In this, that on the ramparts of illusion
Woe breeds war and darker still confusion.
War within each mind, flung out
In agony of conflict long confined
To slay internal tension. Hence aggression,
Certainty of purpose to heal doubt:
'Let me kill others, leaving but my mind,
So shall the field of war be my possession!'
Yet other is but me, to fail or win;
Two hands that wrestle, halves within one whole,
With level vision careless of the sky.
There, even as about, below, within
The pale beyond of our imagining
Is war in quietude; the heart's control
Of twoness; wide awareness, thoughts awing
Of now; and love, the circle infinite
That born of darkness is the light.

Desire

I cried aloud to God, that stood in fire.
But God, it seemed, had heard of my desire
Before,
And as he played upon the floor
His children all about him, said,
Nor raised his head,
'Well, why not drop it?'

This was a self-purge which did me good.

Ideals

Into the endless spaces of the night,
Uplifted with a self-consuming fire,
The rocket starward leaps and in its flight
Symbols the violence of my desire.
I weary of this clay-besotted world;
I scorn the misery miscalled delight.
With naked will tempestuously hurled
To heaven I dominate the proudest height
And on the ramparts of the dawn unfurled
Fling wide the banner of a nobler Plan,
With Truth and Love and Purity empearled,
To sing the grandeur of the Soul of Man . . .
'Tis folly—for no vision comes to birth
Save where the rocket redescends, on earth.

Life

To know there's nothing changeless, that the past
A blind begetter, fathers the pregnant hour;
To say of joy and pain that none will last;
Of opportunity, its womb is power;
Of earth, it is not low; of heaven above,
Its splendour vaults the caverns of the heart;
To know the dumb sweet agony of love;
To say, here's Now, let it be wed with laughter
Till envious death or tedious life doth part,
(There'll never be, there never was hereafter);
To find the rebel at the heart of war,
Compassion; to have found and loved one friend;
Here's any man's enough, with this for more,
To know that life's a journey, but it has no end.

All that is Done

All that is done has died, is dead.
Thought, that of life so lightly wrought
The soon unloved and bartered robe of things,
Our cold and spent imaginings,
Dies in the hour when life and substance wed.

The river of life has no rememberings.
A truth embodied falls to the river bed.
Life on the heart's uprising wings
Flows onward, outward, soars and sings,
Floods the loud orbit of the earth and sky
With turmoil of immediacy.
No thing shall stay that onward flow
And every self, resistant, still shall know
The wounds of suffering and die
Nor stain the lightless fields of memory.

The past, by mind from matter bred
Is but a cold museum of the dead.

Empty the Mind

Empty the mind, of the laden sad illusion
That you and I, regardant each to each
Are other, separate, apart,
Blind to the love-lit splendour of the heart
That lights the grey dark of the world's confusion.

Empty the mind, of tangled knots of hate;
The fear of life and wounding circumstance;
And low desire that grasps importunate
And handles empty shadows; of the will
That shouts of self yet soon or late
Must purge its folly in the fires of ill.

Now fill the voided realms of heart and mind
With all the host of heaven. Add the tears
Of men and healing laughter. Look, and find
No corner where the heart once bled
By joy and splendour now untenanted.

And sing. A free heart knows no fearing.
Wisdom and love, the children of pure sound,
Empty of purpose now, as light appearing,
Shine and are glad, with music crowned.

Onward

The falling tide of darkness flows away.
The voice of self is stilled.
I am a child with opened eyes of day,
A vessel yet unfilled.

I am alone, yet seek not any friend.
I feel the heart of woe.
The face is veiled of my appointed end,
Yet this I know:

The future lies unmoulded in my hands.
A Path winds out before.
There is no backward way. Behind me stands
A closèd door.

Self is a subject of perennial fascination. 'Look within,' says The Voice of the Silence, *'thou art Buddha.' 'I and my Father are one,' said Jesus the Christ. But such experience is rare. I find the threefold self of St Paul, of body, soul and spirit, the most helpful brief analysis, and I seem to have written many poems to say so. The following five are examples.*

Vision

There was a shining wind upon the hill
A sudden wind that brightened all the air.
And I was purified, made free
Made luminous and passionless until,
Of self itself divinely unaware
We ran, the wind and I, with sudden glee
Down to the undivided sea.

I rose, and moving integral I stood,
The hills above me and the sea below.
But there were heights as yet unwon
For evil lusted at the heels of good
And hate made echo in the deeps of woe;
Illusion boasted of a journey done . . .
I let them fall, and lo! the sun.

And then I saw, below yet here I saw
The myriad earth in motion. Trees and men;
Then no more trees and men, or sound
Of difference, but one, that to a law
Of its own being slow revolved, and then
The trees were trees again, and soon I found
That men were men, with splendour crowned.

I looked towards the sky, and it was here,
And all creation as a golden stream
Ran singing down, and turned, a wide
And clouded river. Half it rose, and fear
Lay on the sullen waters with a gleam
Of stillness, for at navel depth it died,
And woman-man was crucified.

The earth and air gave patient audience,
(The eyes above, the feet nailed to the clay).
The waters moved, and from the night
Came life, self-conscious and aware, immense
And jewelled with the lamps of night and day.
And self was on the median way, with light
And dark the mirror ways of sight.

I struggled and desire held me, cried
Aloud and self alone made answering.
I suffered, knew the bonds of hell
Then rose upon the waters sanctified.
I sang and heard the choirs of heaven sing.
And then a voice, cool as a temple bell,
'Thou fool! That way the angels fell.'

There was a shining wind upon the hill,
A sudden wind that brightened all the air.
And I that know my bonds am free,
A sworded regent at the throne of will,
Of Self itself divinely more aware.
We ran, the wind and I with sudden glee
That shed, for just a moment, me.

Thoughts on Self

Self is a folly of the thinking mind,
A thing, thought-made,
And we are blind in our imagining.

The fool, raising a seeking head,
Perceives and yearns with red desire.
Hands follow, craving to acquire
And grasp, themselves already dead.
('Be humble and remain entire').
The self, extruding from the Whole,
With knives of separation damns the soul.

The self is nought, a puppet filled with fear,
A swimmer set to violate the stream;
A voice the wakened Self must bear
Or wake the dreamer from his foolish dream.

The universe is total, whole of will,
Unblemished harmony, and we,
Essential through eternity are still
Unsevered parts of void totality.

SELF is. The Self, awake yet torn,
Strives riven-hearted to let fall
The weight of difference. (The All
Is partless, absolute, Unborn).

O SELF, that self in Self would die,
That Self, of all distinction free
Might slay forever, joyously
The fond, offensive thought of I!

A Song of Self

Oh Self is One, and Two, and Three.
    How foolish to deny!
And all are born of Mind/No-Mind
    And all of them must die.

The worst of me, the beast of Me
    Is child of thought-desire.
It claims and names a severed life;
    It lies about the liar.

The middle me, which on the Wheel
    Returns from birth to birth
Is God within an animal,
    The Light encased in earth.

As character it is the man
    That suffers weal and woe.
With waking eyes it sudden sees
    The Light mirrored below.

The best of me, the least of Me
    Is Light, the whole as part.
In every man, in life and death
    It is the living heart.

It is not mine; it is not I
    Yet none is I beside!
Here's mystery for all that lives
    Till death itself has died.

                .   .   .

And THAT which IS, the Unborn/born,
    The Void of all begot?
'Tis SELF, and Self, and self itself,
    And not!

Meditation on Self

Be seated, thou, unfettered, free,
The heart's attention poised as third of three.
Now still the mind, nor claim the unceasing flow;
He holds the boundless heaven in fee
Who learns the uttermost command—Let go.
Now seal with cold resolve the doors of sense.
Be still, my son, and seek thine Immanence.

I am not body. I am never ill,
Nor restless, weary, fretful, nor in pain.
I am not hot emotion, nor the will
Which forfeits progress in the name of gain.
I am not thought, the process of the mind
On caging partial truth intent,
Unknowing, for its eyes are blind,

The wings of life beat ever unconfined.
I am not any instrument.
I am.

I am the light that slays the night at dawning.
I am the love that woos its own reward.
I am the slow resolve that wakes at morning,
And sleeps at twilight on a sheathèd sword.

I am the fullness in the wealth of giving.
I am the void within the orb of fame.
I am the death that dies within the living.
I am the namelessness that bears the Name.

I am the golden joy of beauty.
I am the stillness underlying sound.
I am the voice of undistinguished duty.
I am the Self in which the self is drowned.

At a Buddhist Funeral

Here nothing is; only a worn-out thought,
Whose parent Mind thinks elsewhere thoughts anew.
Here's but the ashes of a garment wrought
With mental fingers by the living you.

Life only is, Life the unceasing womb,
Whose children move the cycle of their day
And jest a while; within the closing tomb
There's nought but dust new-settled by the Way.

The world is but a grave wherein we find
Only the drifting shadows of Pure Mind.

REBIRTH

As a doctrine this seems to me as obviously true as the fact that life is the same one Life in all its forms. But 'I hear he's Died Again' was, when it came to me, a new way of looking at it.

When I am Dead

When I am dead, who dies, who dies,
    And where am I?
A dewdrop in a shining sea,
    An inmate in the sky?
Or do I rest awhile and thence
Return for new experience?

There's nothing changeless, heaven or hell
    Nor life's oblivion;
Only a heart at rest and then
    A further walking on.
We live and as we live we learn;
We die, and then again return.

Yet who returns, what comes again
    To fretful earth?
I know not. Only this I know;
There is a road that comes to birth
In everyman, and at the end
Each man shall know all life his friend.

Youth in Age

The twilight falls. Inevitable hands
Draw the soft curtains of the fading day.
All changes, grows, grows old. Nature demands

A cycle absolute of growth-decay.
Birth follows, of the flesh, and every hour
The wakening mind, when limbs of courage leap
To fresh awareness, widens, bursts in flower
Awhile in splendour, till the body's sleep.

So life, resistless, strides upon the hills
Of our becoming and with laughing tread
Creates and uses and in using kills,
Till every form with force of life lies dead.

The dissolution of recurring night
Awaits the body. For the spirit, light.

I hear he's Died Again

'I hear he's died again. It had to be
Though choice of circumstance was his alone.'

'You mean that we have lived before, that we
His fellow men have met and truly known
The substance of his yesterday?'
                                        'His life
Is of the One Life; all you see is wrought
Of feeling, thought and act in needful strife
Of self-becoming, for the Way is nought
But of our choosing, and we meet and part
Obedient to effect.'
                        'The new is strange
To memory.'
                        'Of some, and yet the heart,
New-lighted by the Changeless beyond change
Knows that we love and die and live again
In forms of our alone devising. Blind
As yet and bound in self-engendered pain
The foolish man with unawakened mind
Creates himself and strives to rob the Whole

With phantom forms of an immortal soul.'

'Then hands of prayer are raised to heaven in vain?'

'There's only Buddha-Mind or Self or THIS
The Namelessness where death itself is slain.
One Life that dies not; forms that ever die.
Here's hell of loss or fullness of pure bliss
Till, purged of error neither shall remain.'

'So here is grief repeated? Each return
But recognition and a long good-bye?'

'Such is the Wheel whereon we sadly learn.
Such is the Law. We ask but know not why.
Only I know I loved my brother I,
And now I hear that he has died again.'

*Zen Buddhism as a school with its unique purpose was born in China in
the eighth century A.D. Its sole concern, direct personal experience of
the beyond of relativity, of Non-duality, has an increasing fascination
for the Western mind, but it does not lend itself to description. 'Zen-do'
was written after a week-end of meditation in a Zen monastery in Kyoto.
Before I left Japan, in September 1946, Dr D. T. Suzuki, the greatest
authority on Zen in modern times, wrote to me about a collection of
material I was packing to bring home. In his letter he referred to this
poem: 'It is fine, and beautifully it illustrates the Zen spirit of Eternal
Now, and All in One and One in All. You are a good poet.' I can only
bow in silence before such praise.*

Zen-do

Silence, and a far-sounding bell.
No words, which broken-winged presume,
Themselves of caged flight, to tell
The beyond of our imagining.
Two slow-descending points illume
The graven stillness. In each cell,
The locked unmoving body, shines

The white flame of a thought awing,
And only the riven heart confines
The ambit of our travelling.

There's no remembrance here, no leaping thought
With eager feet pursuing the unknown.
Desire, and all the fretful folly wrought
Of earth's incessant fancy, sleeps. Alone
The flame which lights the manifold is one.
The universe, contracted and confined,
Dwells in the compass of a bounded mat.
The pale flame in the passion-voided mind
Purges the difference of this and that.
No purpose here, nor time-ascending vow
To stain the moment absolute of Now.

The many and the one. The mind ascends
Twin-footed to the ladder's end, and finds
Unmeasured union. But nothing ends,
And though the sun-flame all consuming blends
The many millioned candles of our minds
In larger union, there's one, and I
That hold it so, and these regardant twain
Impatient cry for larger unity,
And the wheel, contentless, turns and swings again.

The pale candle, reason, droops and dies
And to the low-lit pentagon of sense
Comes beauty, veil-less, naked of the lies
Which foul with argument our dull pretence
Of knowing, and with fingers of delight
Fondles the tentacles of touch and sight.

And here, with eyes of laughter, is the face
Of love, young love, still rosy warm and fair
With the unestimated bold embrace
Of life, and a wild flower in her hair.
Then reason wakens, rude to her caress,
And proves upon the square of reckoning

That all is gilt illusion, love no less;
And I am sick of a wild thought, to fling
To rot in some unmeasurable pit
All sound of beauty and the touch of it.

Now let the unravished heart arise, and find
Communicable light. If all is one,
And all diversity the spawn of mind,
Then madly was this mocking wheel begun.
If in the falling water of the hills
I hear but loved illusion; if the sun
By day on proffered breast and thigh instils
No cherished warming, night no benison,
Then life is but a lie that's told too long,
And love is dead, and in the heart no song.

I will not have it so. Be still my heart.
I will arise, and splendid grasp the whole,
And binding it about yet hold each part
Unutterably so; approve the soul
And substance of the rose, and lightly bring
Eternal glory to the littlest thing.
And each, the part and whole, shall singing dwell
In each inseverable. Not one but two,
The sound of wholeness, and the sounding bell.
And every leaf which unreported grew,
And some time in some other planet fell
Is still the abundant absolute, and grows
Unlabelled on the divine slopes of hell,
Nor cares that it is hemlock or the rose.

I sought for truth, and waking now I find
That there is neither truth nor waking mind.
Yet each exists, supreme, immaculate
Uniquely one, alone companionate.
At last I know, who feel the risen sun.
Awake, my heart! For two is two, and one!

I rose, and passed into the morning, where
The garden rose in stillness, and the light

Gave benediction to the silvering air.
The flowing hills passed onward, and the night
Her velvet fallen, moved upon their flow,
And suddenly and utterly, 'twas day.
I knelt, the flowers about me, kneeling low
Where the starlit dew, night's holy water, lay
And all about my wakened eyes was new
And soft the dawn wind, and the dew was dew.

I rose and moved upon the way
   And in my heart a song;
And what the singing heart shall say
   Has never yet been wrong.
And this I know, and sing I must
   Of all that I have found;
That every grain of dust is dust
   And the wheels of a cart go round.

The remaining poems are not specifically Buddhist, nor is my interest in poetry, but nature, love and war are themes of perennial interest to the poet.

Seagulls

Over the wide and windy shores
   In splendour flying
Cresting the billows of an airy sea
With silver wingèd sails a-lee
Or windward beating majesty,
And ever the song that knows no pause
   A pale autumnal crying.

At dusk, when on the sea-flung wall
   The day is dying;
When dawn awakes, and soon the sun
The battle of the night has won;

When evening sheds her benison,
Ever the grey unearthly call
A pale autumnal crying.

When soft the windless waters flow
In slumber sighing;
Or when the sea in wild affray
Comes foaming with a vast array
In serried grandeur of display,
Ever the keening voice of woe
A pale autumnal crying.

Though far the English heart may roam
The foe defying
Yet faint upon that alien ground
Wherever English hearts are found
This muted melody of sound
Will echo of the shores of home,
The seagulls' crying, crying . . .

The Hills of Connemara

There is a land where a mountain flings
Its amethyst and azure wings
Twelve pointed to the sky.
Where the sweep of the hills is emerald blue
And the vales of scented heather woo
The winter-wearied eye.

Where a mountain's tears go rolling down
In sunlit ripples amber-brown
And a laughing stream is born.
And which is the lovelier none can say
The bloom on the hills at the close of day
Or the light on the hills at dawn.

This poem was conceived when looking from a St John's Wood bedroom window, but it was written entirely in my car between the house and the City. The lines were composed as I drove and written down in traffic blocks. This clearly proves something or other. Or does it?

London Dawn

Darkness entire, the velvet dark of sleep
All light close-curtained in oblivion
All beings void of least communion
Lost in a wide unknowing, shallow-deep.

Night's immanence, as yet bereft of words
And the sad wilderness of human fret
Divides and sudden wakes, to silence set
To music by the love-lit song of birds.

Now dawn, shy-footed in dissolving gloom,
In trespass at the tomb of night declares
Allegiance to the rose and proudly shares
The grace and perfume of awakening bloom.

The panoply of night is laid away;
The cycle slow revolves and it is day.

Lines in Firelight

Now is the twilight of our yet becoming
When light, that glows in cloud and shadow
As in golden day, in aspiration yet unsung
And in our least imagining
Is seen with eyes no longer veiled
In fond desiring, nor confined
In scope to the wrought images
That bound and bind Reality.

Softly, as music falls on our remembrance,
Light, from the live and comfortable fire
Illumines for the heart's caress the forms
Of beauty gathered to the self,
And proffers each to contemplation;
Light, the eyes of life, that with the falling years
No less in splendour shines in the earth lamps
Of our embodiment.

Content in that repose of action when the will
Forgoing purpose kneels obedient,
Of such is peace, in leisured limb, in mind
The long day's burden shed, in heart
That, sharing a still, unformed awareness
Sees its life-beloved, the inseverable other
Lovelit, there.

How Great is Your Beloved?

How great is your Beloved? Mine
    Is margined only with the final star.
His feet are on the homely shores,
Washed with the lees of cobalt wine
Where to and fro the siren moon indraws
The tumult of the sea, and slow
The moonled waters' tidal flow
Comes surging from afar.

Green are the limbs of my Beloved. Trees,
With feathery plumes and column'd dignity,
Where soft the busy twilight breeze
Makes elfin music. Through the night
Brown shoulders move in solemn dance
With weaving arms of suppliance
And whisper to the stars in ecstacy
Of delicate delight.

His heart is in the hills. Serene
He dwells amid the luminous proud air.
The ramparts of His splendour lean
In combat with the wind, and wear
The crown of silence. Proud, the ermine snow
Mantles the breast of night. Blue dyed
The valley mist, and soft below
The bells of eventide.

His eyes are in the light, and see
The humbler visions of the heart made whole.
The moon upon his breast is laid,
The sun his flaming aureole.
And I, of wholeness unafraid,
Of all His Love the lowliest littlest part
Lie singing in the boundless Me
Close curled about His heart.

*Written in bed one Easter Sunday morning in the country. Why I know
not, but it is commendably quotable.*

Make me no Vows

Make me no vows, that through the untrodden years
You'll love with naked heart no other man.
Make me no vows, nor tangle me with tears.
We met, and now we part, as we began.

You gave me love and joy and true befriending
And all your beauty and the deeps of mind,
And now that love, our joyous love, is ending
We'll kiss and part, and nothing leave behind.

We wove the pattern of our days in laughter,
In body's rapture and the heart's delight.
Content, we gave no thought to love's hereafter;
Love, when the day is fair, forgets the night.

When first I lay, your body's beauty given,
With tired eyes upon your cooling breast
The velvet of your limbs, your hands, was heaven
And mine the quiet of the heart's unrest.

I never stained that stillness with enquiring
Nor turned the handle of a closèd door.
It was enough that I was then desiring
And you were smiling, and I asked no more.

And now that for a while our love is ended,
Its splendour faded as a robe outworn,
The ramparts of our pride once more defended,
Make me no vows to bind the days unborn.

Let there be neither vows nor vain regretting.
Passion deplores the key-rings of the heart.
Brief was our love, and sweet beyond forgetting.
We met. We loved a little. Now we part.

Farewell

Speak not, beloved, for thy voice would wound
The fleeting moment's deep solemnity.
Let silence reign. Oft, in the common round
Of parting, words have bruised the frailty
Of such a silence as transcended sound.

Words may be tender, moving, passionate,
So splendidly employed that grief is drowned
Beneath love's eloquence, but soon or late
The god-like majesty of speech is crowned
With silence. So let this our silence tell
The measure of our love. Fling wide thy soul,
And bind the feet of time in such a spell
That all the sleeping earth from pole to pole
Will here be present. So, when I depart,
I shall not leave the ambit of thy heart
But still be with thee when I say—farewell.

POEMS IN WARTIME

I am not alone in looking back on the war years with surprise at the emotions then produced. There was little anger, no doubt at all about the result, and because of the sense of commonweal and purpose many of us, in spite of six months' bombing, were actually happy as seldom since. If 'June, 1940', the date of Dunkirk, is slightly hysterical so perhaps were we. 'You had to go', written from the woman's point of view, rouses emotion as I read it even today. It happened all too often.

On our return to London from the South of France in August 1939 we stayed as usual for a night at Chartres. They were removing and burying the priceless windows.

South Portal, Chartres

Deep graven with a nameless hand,
Severely tall, immeasurably calm
Unknown to man's intemperate alarm
You understand
With patient comprehending eyes
The tears of seven centuries.

These eyes have seen the soul of France
In battle born, slow tempered with distress,
Bloom with the lily's prideful loveliness.
Yet sword and lance,
Inturned as some deliberate goad,
Have ever stained the unfinished road.

You do not speak, yet in your ken
Lies garnered wisdom old ere Satan fell,
And from those lips a burdened voice might tell
Why foolish men
May live and love yet will to slay
Their fellow pilgrims on the Way.

August 1939

June, 1940

Now stands the heart of England true revealed.
All lesser loves departed, laid aside,
Washed clean of hate, with sorrow purified,
There's never doubt nor hurt but now is healed
With resolution, native born,
To march the length of night, and live to see
With quiet eyes the inevitable morn,
Or, in the hour's necessity
To die, lest England yield.

The heart of England, deathless, will prevail.
Not with a sword of words, nor proud display;
Only a dull resolve in the English way
Lest in the agony of proof we fail.

If there's a price to pay of English tears
Of garnered gold, of toil, or homes aflame
We'll pay, and on the honour of our name
Stamp the receipt in splendour. All our fears
Are fallen, all illusion shed.
Shall freedom live, or lie below the heel
Of darkness? There's the gauntlet proffered, red
With innocence, of bloodied steel;
Now England's glove appears.

The lists are open with the world as field.
The wounds of doubt with cold resolve are healed.
Now stands the heart of England true revealed;
We fight, until we fall. We shall not yield.

In Temple Gardens

One window left, for shuttered gloom
　　Lies fast on many a folded eye.
Yet still within my shadowed room
　　The trees, the flowers, the open sky

Lay healing hands upon a mind
  Of quietude by war bereft.
Wherefore I toil content who find
  One window left.

The Wild Rose

I heard the young wild roses sing
Where blue the heavens smiled.
And long I stood, slow lingering
With petal mind awondering
And the wide eyes of a child.

I heard the guns in thunder call
And pale the wintry sky.
I saw the rising steeples fall.
I found the human heart in thrall
And none could answer why.

And still the young wild roses sing
Nor pause to make reply.
And still the guns are thundering
  And still the child is wondering.
Who answers it? Not I.

You had to Go

You had to go. It mattered not
That even as you came to birth
Your father's body, face to earth,
Lay shattered in a Flanders field,
His laughing eyes with darkness sealed.
He never saw the son that he begot.

You heard the guns of battle cease
You saw the birth of fretful peace

As through the aftermath of woe
I weaned you in a mist of tears
And watched you grow.
And as you climbed the ascending years
In sunlit joys and shadowed fears,
Swift to engage
In any foolish wild emprise,
I saw within your eager eyes
The light they say that loved to show
Within your father's at your age.
His life in yours again must flow.
I understand. You had to go.

Life was a gay adventure, death
But the ending of a song.
And while the heart held laughter, body breath,
The road was never sad, nor journey long.
No moral problem dimmed your day;
Your right was right, your wrong forgiveless wrong,
And truth and wisdom never dared betray
The cause of England, viewed in the English way.

You gave your life to healing, to the art
That, born of books, yet lies in part
Within the eye that sees the part made whole.
You hated pain, and man's insensate lust
And all that dragged his freedom in the dust,
Assuming for your knightly goal
Damnation to the unjust.
So did your father long ago.
I said no word. I knew you had to go.

Too soon the marching feet of war
Made echo at my closèd door,
Yet haply died away.
But you, with eyes of longing raised
To sunlit wombs of horror, praised
The freedom of the air.
And all too soon in tunic gay

You proudly flew the wings of grey
And called upon me to display
The joy I could not share.
Your father would have had it so.
And I? I knew you had to go.

Yet when those feet, returning, spoke
Of duty to fulfil,
The half-forgotten horror woke
In agony of will.
And I, who should have set aside
In English pride
The tears that bade you stay—
I said but foolish things, and cried
When you too went away.

I saw your father's sudden smile
The night you said good-bye.
You lightly said, 'It's only for a while,'
Believing it, and I,
Hating the sullen need of things,
This parting, and the noisy wings
That filled the autumn sky—
I simply said, 'Let's hope it will be so,'
And bade you go.

Humanity

I saw the nations of the earth as men,
Each of his people's fashioning,
And each unyielding, watching stood
And knew alone their differing.

I saw the nations as a single man
Who tore his striving limbs, and beat
His heart, and moaned and cried aloud,
And the blood ran rivers to his feet.

I saw him grope and sway with blinded eyes
In agony of soul's unease;
Then slow but still resistant fall
Down to unwilling knees.

And there, in sudden wild amaze,
As though a splendour seen afar,
I saw his heart with yearning fill
And, in his opened eyes, a star.

Compassion

I knew the bombing. I was there.
I felt the terror, saw the red blood spilled;
Heard thunder in the flame-lit air,
And running feet that stumbled and were stilled.
I knew the bombing everywhere;
I watched the laws of love and hate fulfilled.
Of all the agony too wide aware
I suffered and was blinded and was killed.

I loved, and loving lived in hell,
I that am whole and still unharmed and well.

I Dreamed that I was Blinded

I dreamed that I was blinded, that the sun
And lesser suns of loveliness were dead.
The flowers smiled no more, their glory shed
And beauty, veiled, denied her benison.
I turned my soul about within my head
And never a sense had further audience.
There was a darkness and a silence now
Whence all but a forgotten faith had fled.
Then slow the clouded gates of immanence

Gave opening, generous to endow
The closèd eye with wisdom yet unread.

There was a sudden splendour and a cry
The music of unutterable song
And lo! The curtains of the inward eye
So wrapt in dark forgetfulness so long
Dissolved and fell away. Reality—
Or so to me it seemed whose sudden wings
Tumultuous uprose in ecstasy—
Blazed with a flame that knew not earth or sky,
But all about me, deep as ocean, strong
As new love, thundered and surged eternally.

Here death was but a garment laid aside.
Eternal principles were living things.
The dotard pendulum of right and wrong
Far from the earth's discordant murmurings
Slept, and the golden Mean was glorified.
And love was over all, horizon wide
Of benison, tremendous, cool, serene
With laughing eyes that viewed a far demesne
Contented, joyous, One, heart-unified.

I woke, and all about the light of day
Clouded the light within. Even the sun
That wakened wide my house of clay
Was darkness to me now, yet as I lay
Bade me remember. I remembered—war
That tedious tale of battles lost or won
Of beauty slain and love's oblivion.

I turned about, and willed to wake no more.
Reality was veiled, but silence spoke.
'There is a light within, a light without.
The light has seven veils; the first is doubt.
Know that the lights are One.'
                                    Again I woke.

Thanksgiving
(For VE Day)

For dawn that follows darkness, for the light
That surges into life with sudden song;
For joy within a heart made newly strong;
For silence in the night
Thank God.

For freedom in the limbs of thought; for eyes
To reap the splendour of a day new born
When hands and thoughts creative greet the morn
And drear destruction dies;
For holidays; for the cry of gulls awing;
For shores unguarded and the sails of peace;
For the benediction of the heart's release
From darkened wondering
Thank God.

For families at one, long riven wide;
For simple friendly things long laid away;
For sleep unfearing at the close of day;
For friends at eventide;
For beauty, shameless in a bold appeal;
For gentleness, no longer penitent;
For idleness that dares to be content;
For the sense of commonweal
Thank God.

I know not who this God may be
Whose shrine is in the inmost me,
Yet humbly with a heart aflame
I murmur to the Nameless Name,
And turning from the days of war
That lead but to the ever less,
With aching eyes invoke the More
That lies beyond that wilderness,
And as I tread the olden Road
That once another Pilgrim trod,
Thank God.

Evensong

I looked in a church for Jesus
As evensong began
And I heard of the God of Jesus
But little of God as man.

I walked out into the sunlight
Where the new and the bygone dead
Are life for the yews and cedars,
Where many a garment shed

Has gone to the earth, its maker,
Till the wearer, robed anew
Comes back for wiser learning
As another me or you.

And there I saw the Gardener
With an olden face and wise.
And in his hands he held a spade
And God was in his eyes.

'They sing within', I said, 'to God
Whoever He may be.
But I shall follow Jesus
Who is God as ideal me.

For if man should live as Jesus
I see no need for God,
For in His eyes were wisdom
And His spade within the sod.'

The Gardener was silent, still,
Then raised a lowly head,
And the sun was level in his eyes
And, 'Jesus died,' he said.

And a bird in the void of stillness
Sang to the setting sun.
And a wild rose fell contented,
And Evensong was done.

Before the war my wife and I were confirmed balletomanes, and our recollection is of dancing, glorious dancing. After the war came symbolism, politics and sociological problems, but little dancing or none as we remembered it. I wrote the following one disappointed evening, sadly.

An English Ballet

I took my heart, my passion to enjoy,
And reason on a laggard lead came after.
I sought for beauty, not for beauty's toy
For rolling humour, not for pleasant laughter.
I said, with patting hands, 'He dances well,
And she is charming, and the music's bright.'
But there was never, never need to quell
The quickening breath, the tumult heart in flight,
Nor live unbreathing as a shaft of light,
A dreaming ecstasy of moonlit white,
In rhythm rose and delicately fell
And danced with naked soul in all men's sight;
Never a silence, holy, vast as night
Then, thunderous, the rich exultant yell
Of uncontrollable delight . . .

Hungry I went, and food there was for mind.
I took my heart. 'Twas better left behind.

If Justice is in fact a woman she must at times be quite intolerably bored at our attempts to serve her. These lines emerged in sympathy one long, hot summer's day.

In the Court of Appeal

Gray faces, and a mist of words. Gray walls
To mould and regulate the law-filled mind
While Justice sits, uncomfortably blind
And voices plead and pray till silence falls
On the last dregs of argument. The Court,
Bright roses in a garden of no flowers,
Incarnate scales to whom the flight of hours
Is weightless as the circle-drift of thought,
Play ball with precedent, distinctions fine
As silk unravelled, views through days expressed
In words debatable.
             A fainting breast
Rose fast and fell as, with a pleading sign
Justice arose and silently withdrawn
Made love to daisies on the Temple lawn.

I do not believe that William Shaksper of Stratford wrote any of the poems or plays of Shakespeare, and for many years I was President of the Shakespearean Authorship Society, whose object is to find who did. I think the most likely poet is the Earl of Oxford. These lines, loaded with allusions to the supporting evidence, were read at a Society Dinner.

Edward de Vere, Earl of Oxford

The earth was shaken with a golden spear
When sonnet, poem and star-revealing play
So burned an altar-heart that men revere
Still wondering, the sun that knew not day.
The mask, the mummer's robe was unremoved;
The world unknowing praised a barren stage.

The lord of England by his Queen beloved
In silence wrote and sealed his heritage.
Men knew him not who, in the human mind
Moved as a god, all frailty forgiven
And proffered to his only heirs, mankind
A hand in darkness on the road to heaven.
Truth ever true will in the end unfold
And even on the breath of pain be told.

Written at Whitsun 1946 in the private house of the late Dr D. T. Suzuki in Kamakura, Japan. The night was too beautiful for sleep.

Kamakura Dawn
For Hilda Leyel in Sussex

How still the light of morning grows
Where maple and the English rose,
Dew lovely to the waking eye
Exalt the heart in sanctuary.

In England, now so long ago
There lies a garden that I know.
And there the rose, her jewelled head
With pale moon-lanterns garlanded,
Yearns with a red-lipped loveliness
Her lover's prodigal caress.
There would I see with shining eyes
Her swift exultant Lord arise,
And watch upon some vacant lawn
The unused miracle of dawn.

Oh, would that I might here forget
The poplars' leaning line; and yet
Some other wind in other trees
Sings now the pale green song of these,

And falls again to sleep. And soon
The blue and breathless mirror, noon
Reflects a living stillness. Deep
The golden silence of that sleep;
Only the falling waters dare
Make music on the listening air.

The timeless cryptomeria throws
Its cooling blessing o'er the rose;
The slow descending arc of day
Lays shadowed velvet on the way
Where hope and joy and all our fears
Climb far the worn ways of the years.

In England at the journey's end
Of day, the light and darkness blend,
And linger in the scented lane
As lovers will that meet again.

Your friends, each others' friends, would move
Content as those who fear not love,
And gather for the by and by
The chosen flowers of memory,
Pressing the moonlit hours away
Indifferent to the unborn day.

Here the unhelpful night-wind soon
Draws busy veils about the moon
And heat, a leaden burden, lies
Unwilling on the fretful eyes.
The laggard rays of day embark
And fade before the relentless dark,
And night, upon the land and sea
Assumes her lightless majesty.

Yet even as I sleep, with you
Nature and man alike pursue
Their sunlit purposes, until

The unpurposed Wheel shall slow fulfil
Each voided, unreturning hour
And night, a night of June, the dark flower
Of an English heaven, slow draws on
The smooth robe of oblivion.

And I in Kamakura stand
Serene within an alien land
For night among these warrior men
Is strong with the strong thought of Zen.
The silence deepens in the drowned
And breathless air, and the far sound
Of waters on a wind-born sea
Is echo to old memory.
I dream as over all the earth
Each home-returning heart gives birth,
O'erleaping the flung span of space,
To some beloved, unfading face.
I dream, and I am far away,
And here, unheeded, it is day.

My longest poem, and perhaps a fragment of spiritual autobiography. As first published it lacked the last two lines, but an elderly Buddhist friend, puzzled, said, 'So there is no beyond?' I tore my hair and added a couplet.

Beyond
A Metaphysical Enquiry

Beyond the compass of the day, beyond
The unfettered flight of rising thought, which sings
And soars, wide-throated in delight, with bliss
Of bright awareness; utterly beyond
The wildest reach of far imagining,
Is what? The mind expands, intolerant
Of all unknowing, builds and nobly dreams

Of ultimates of bold infinity;
In vain. The stallions of enquiry storm
The blue-lit fields of high philosophy
In vain. Thought falters, founders in despair,
With empty hands admitting impotence.

Science; the word is stuffed with arrogance.
The power of mind; here's thought gone mad with self.
The heart; here's better bludgeon for the door
That bars Reality. Frail water slow
Dissolves the living and tremendous rock
Into oblivion. Shall the heart with soft
Relentless will consume the rampart walls
Of self, the folly self? Here's hope in vain;
For thought and feeling, twins of reasoning
Spring from the loins of dull duality.
Not this, not with a weapon in the hand
That thrusts at something other, not with two
In bitter contest is this battle won,
But sudden, when the friend is foe and each
Dissolved in each, ceases to be.
                                                What then?

What notches cut to climb, what rising path
To fresh awareness? How to *know* beyond
All acquisition, loss or difference?
The printed word is but a burden now,
Speech but a sound unmeaning on the air.
Not here, not there, but somewhere, casket-hidden,
Truth, ere man arose to seek, ere time
Had semblance, *is*, unmoving, unconfined . . .

It is within. Here's heart of all enquiry.
Here, not at the goal of far adventure,
Now, not in the long convenience of time;
And doing this, though this be pale of worth
And fruitless to mankind. It flames, it shines,
A light-house light that in the hands of will
Burns with awareness . . .

Such is fancy still;
Projected image on projected screen;
Here's nought to see of true experience.
Still the machine of thought is sounding. Still,
Recording nothing worth, the folded sheets
Of knowledge clatter through. What function, then,
What process of im-mediate consciousness
Shall tear the mask from seeming, break each mould
And thus let life, all body shed, be free?

It is the voice of Truth invisible,
A lamp in every human mind, the light
That glows upon the darkling road to heaven.
It knows the substance of beyond, and shines
In darkness, downward, to illume the sad
Arena of our proud self-consciousness;
And up, a searchlight in the sun, with rays
Of pure experience. By this alone
We know direct, as one who sudden looks
Into the face of God and, letting fall
The burden, loses self-awareness. Reason
Then, refused the final view may yet
Create a desperate ladder to the height,
And, even as the feet that climb let fall
The steps of their arrival, so shall thought
Be servant to a nobler faculty
In forfeit of attainment. Let us climb.

Life is of THAT—we know It not, nor shall—
The Namelessness, the Void, God's Father. Men
Have mouthed a thousand names for It, nor stained
It with the sound. We see the robes that clothe
Its first becoming, attributes of power
And such dimension as the strutting mind
Can fold about Infinity. We cry,
With folded hands of pitiful demand
And desperate invocation. Yet we know—
And here's an infant candle in the night
Of ignorance—that all that breathes is part

And child of this magnificence. If, then,
(The voice of thought breaks in with argument)
The Absolute is knowable as One
And in the One the ceaseless manifold,
Shall not the littlest part of Wholeness see,
Attain, become the like Divinity?

Alas that thought has no such knowing. Thought,
Which measures, tears each petal from the rose
Whose loveliness, intangible as dawn
Laughs at the scalpel of enquiry. Thought
Proclaims, and splendidly, that 'Thou art THAT'
Yet utter fails to see the Darkness–Light
Made visible. Be humble now; the eye
Intuitive has no dimensions, knows
And absolutely, sees with instant power
Of eyeless vision—suddenly to see,
Direct, none seeing, utterly aware.

Beyond—the word is failing. Now the Truth
Exultant as a rocket, shatters the gates
Of wonder. There's no heaven yonder save
The heaven here, no hell but evil wrought
Of man's devising. There is nought beyond!

Thus Wisdom throned in self-identity,
In non-duality of earth and heaven,
Burns and blends and fuses all that's two
And in their suchness sees them utterly
At once divided-indivisible.
Wisdom expands; Compassion, as a flower
That, delicately waking, swells from bud
To blossom in the warm and love-lit air,
With swift, consummate skill-in-means commands
A thousand forms of helpfulness. Wisdom-
Compassion, each the majesty of each,
Twin pulses of the heart of being, grow
In fusion of dissolved communion.

Where reason falters, discord in a surge
Of meaning shatters the pregnant stillness
Into sudden joy. So Truth, with noise
Of merriment explodes the One, scatters
A thousand petals on the laughing air
And thunders in the streets of our illusion.
The tempest shrivels. There is utter light
In silence visible. A vast content
Made luminous consumes awareness. Thought,
Bereft of purpose, lightless, impotent
Abandons effort in a wild despair.
The search is ended; there is no beyond;
Save in the vast immeasurable bliss,
Beyond beyond, of here and now and this.

GEORGE ALLEN & UNWIN LTD

Head Office
40 Museum Street, London W.C.1
Telephone: 01–405 8577

Sales, Distribution and Accounts Departments
Park Lane, Hemel Hempstead, Herts.
Telephone: 0442 3244

Athens: 7 Stadiou Street
Barbados: P.O. Box 222, Bridgetown
Beirut: Deeb Building, Jeanne d'Arc Street
Bombay: 103/5 Fort Street, Bombay I
Calcutta: 285J Bepin Behari Ganguli Street, Calcutta 12
Delhi: 1/18 B Asaf-Ali Road, New Delhi I
Ibadan: P.O. Box 62
Karachi: Karachi Chambers, McLeod Road
Lahore: 22 Falettis Hotel, Egerton Road
Madras: 2/18 Mount Road, Madras
Mexico: Villalongin 32, Mexico 5, D.F.
Nairobi: P.O. Box 30583
Philippines: P.O. Box 157, Quezon City D-502
Singapore: 248c-6 Orchard Road, Singapore 9
Sydney N.S.W.: Bradbury House, 55 York Street
Tokyo: C.P.O. Box 1728, Tokyo 100–91
Ontario: 2330 Midland Avenue, Agincourt
Wellington: P.O. Box 1467, Wellington, New Zealand